ER
4IR

Glow-in-the-Dark ANIMALS

Written by Kris Hirschmann

Illustrated by Jean Cassels

Copyright © 2000 by Troll Communications L.L.C.

Planet Reader is an imprint of Troll Communications L.L.C.

All rights reserved. No part of this book may be reproduced or utilized in any form or by any means, electronic or mechanical, including photocopying, recording, or by any information storage and retrieval system, without written permission from the publisher.

Printed in the United States of America.   ISBN 0-8167-6947-8

10 9 8 7 6 5 4 3 2 1

Welcome to Planet Reader!

Invite your child on a journey to a wonderful, imaginative place—the limitless universe of reading! And there's no better traveling companion than you, the parent. Every time you and your child read together you send out an important message: Reading can be rewarding and *fun*. This understanding is essential to helping your child build the skills and confidence he or she needs as an emerging reader.

Here are some tips for sharing Planet Reader stories with your child:

Be open! Some children like to listen to or read the whole story and then ask questions. Some children will stop on every page with a question or a comment. Either way is fine; the most important thing is that your child feels reading is a pleasurable experience.

Be understanding! Sometimes your child might need a direct answer. If he or she points to a word and asks you to tell what it is, do so. Other times, your child may want to sound out a word or stop to figure out a sentence independently. Allow for both approaches.

Enjoy! This book was created especially for your child's age group. Talk about the story. Take turns reading favorite parts. Look at how the illustrations support the story and enhance the reading experience.

And most of all, enjoy your child's journey into literacy. It's one of the most important trips the two of you will ever take!

You may have seen blinking yellow lights in the air on a warm summer evening. The lights come from little beetles called *fireflies*. Fireflies are *bioluminescent* (BY-oh-loo-mi-NESS-sent). This means they can glow.

Fireflies are the most familiar bioluminescent animals. But they are far from the only ones. Many other creatures can make their own light. Some are found on land. But most live in the ocean.

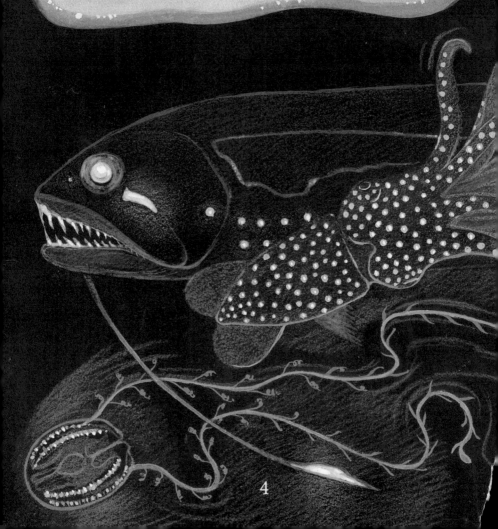

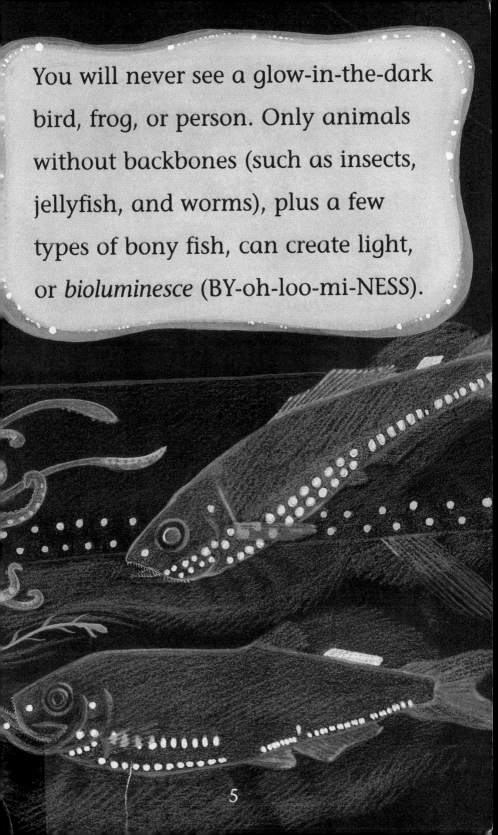

You will never see a glow-in-the-dark bird, frog, or person. Only animals without backbones (such as insects, jellyfish, and worms), plus a few types of bony fish, can create light, or *bioluminesce* (BY-oh-loo-mi-NESS).

Animals "turn on" their lights by mixing two chemicals: *luciferin* (loo-SIH-fur-in) and *luciferase* (loo-SIH-fur-ays). When these chemicals combine, they glow. The glow is usually blue, blue-green, or white, but it can be many other colors.

Unlike lightbulbs, fires, and most other light sources, *bioluminescence* (BY-oh-loo-mi-NESS-ens) creates no heat. For this reason it is sometimes called *cold light*. You can hold a glowing creature, such as a firefly, in your hand without fear of being burned.

Bioluminescent animals use their light in many different ways. Some use it to see. Others use it to scare away predators. Still others use it to attract prey.

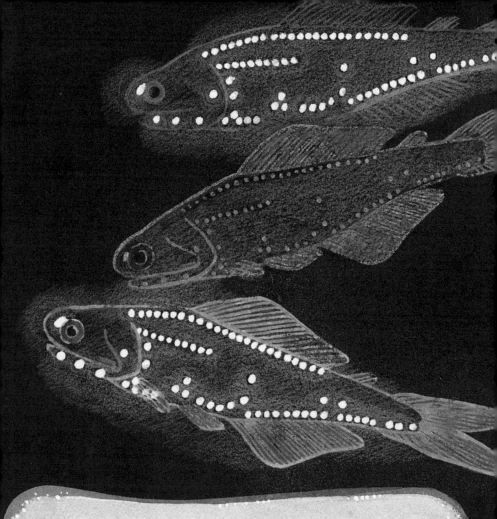

A few animals have a special use
for their glow. These animals send
signals to other members of the
same group by blinking their lights
and moving their bodies in just the
right way. It's like a secret code!

The smallest glowing animals are called *dinoflagellates* (DY-no-FLA-juh-lets). These one-celled creatures live in the ocean. They swim by waving whiplike tails.

Dinoflagellates stay dark most of the time. But if they are moved around, they create tiny blue sparks.

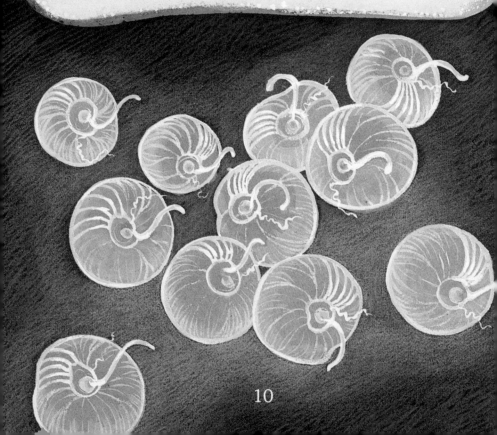

When millions of dinoflagellates gather, they can make the water glow. In some parts of the world, boats and swimmers are followed by eerie blue-green trails. And off the California coast, breaking waves sometimes shine at night.

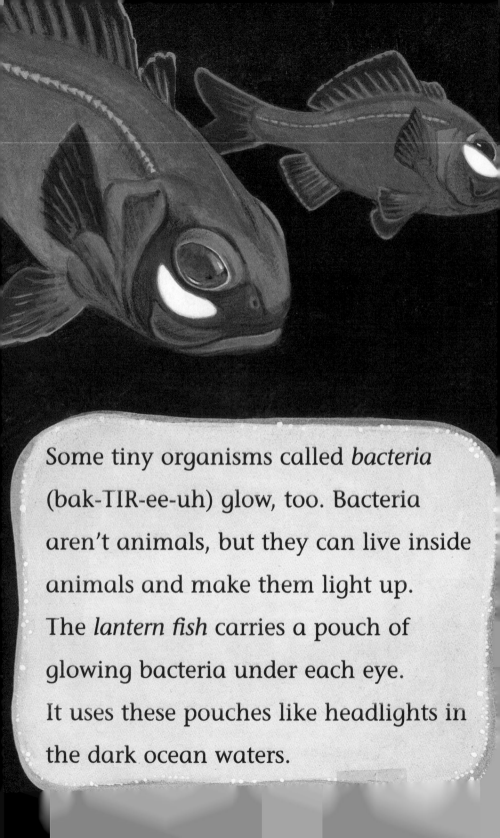

Some tiny organisms called *bacteria* (bak-TIR-ee-uh) glow, too. Bacteria aren't animals, but they can live inside animals and make them light up. The *lantern fish* carries a pouch of glowing bacteria under each eye. It uses these pouches like headlights in the dark ocean waters.

The *angler fish* lives far below the sea's surface. It dangles a sac filled with glowing bacteria in front of its toothy mouth. When small creatures approach the glowing sac, they are quickly gobbled up by the hungry predator.

In the ocean, little sunlight reaches deeper than 800 feet (244 m). Many creatures live in these cold, dark depths, and most of them glow. One odd-looking deep-water hunter is the *viperfish*. This animal's mouth is full of lights—as many as 350 of them! When the viperfish opens its mouth, prey swims right in.

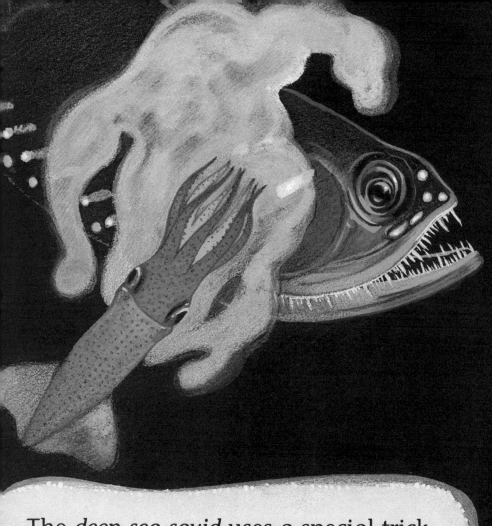

The *deep-sea squid* uses a special trick to escape danger. It squirts a cloud of glowing ink at its attacker. The shining blob confuses the predator long enough for the squid to get away.

Not all glow-in-the-dark ocean dwellers lurk in the deep. Some live near the surface, where they can be easily seen.

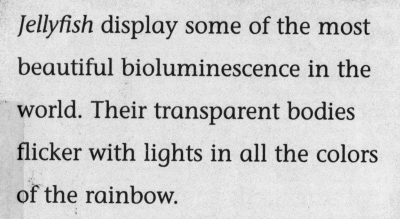

Jellyfish display some of the most beautiful bioluminescence in the world. Their transparent bodies flicker with lights in all the colors of the rainbow.

Jellyfish use their lights like burglar alarms. If a jellyfish is attacked, its lights flash brightly. The attacker usually swims away, afraid that a bigger predator might come to explore.

The *firefly squid* brightens the seas around Japan each spring. This 4-inch (10-cm) animal is covered with flashing blue-white lights. Not only is the firefly squid beautiful, it is tasty. Its glow helps other animals to find it and to catch it.

The *cookie-cutter shark,* which measures just 12 inches (30 cm), has a glowing belly. From below, the shark looks bright, not dark. This helps it to "disappear" when the sun is out. Predators swimming underneath have a tough time spotting this shiny fellow!

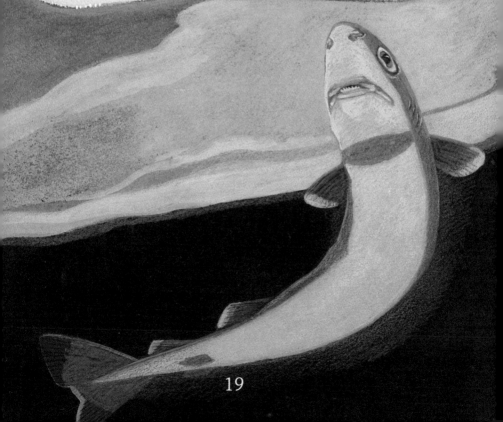

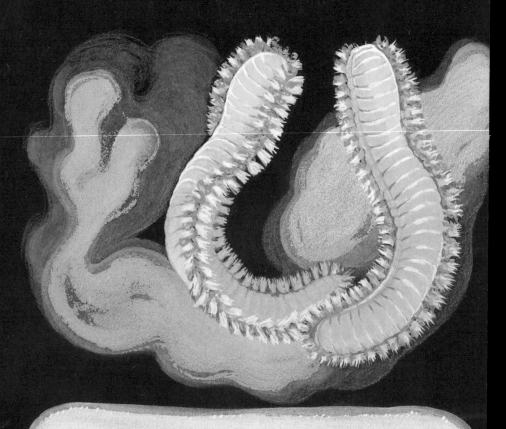

At night, shallow coral reefs light up with bioluminescence. *Fire worms* don't usually glow. But three or four times a year, these reef dwellers put on a show. With their bodies glowing bright blue-green, they swim to the surface and perform a fiery dance to attract other worms.

A tiny clamlike creature called the *sea firefly* lives on ocean floors around Japan. At night, it swims to the surface to feed. If disturbed, it glows bright blue and swims away, leaving a glowing trail behind.

The *brittle star* is an amazing reef dweller. This starfish has a round body and five long arms. It can glow green. The brittle star has a clever way of protecting itself. If it is attacked, this animal will drop one of its arms. The glowing arm distracts the attacker. Then the brittle star goes dark and crawls away. Later, the missing arm grows back.

There are some interesting glow-in-the-dark animals on land, too.

The *railroad worm* of South America is a beetle larva. It is special because it glows green and red! The railroad worm has red lights on its head and green lights down each side of its body. Most bioluminescent animals glow in only one color.

When lit, a railroad worm looks like a tiny train moving through the night. Its red lights are like headlights on a car, and its green lights look like windows. That's how this animal got its name.

Thousands of *glowworms* blanket the roof of Glowworm Grotto in Waitomo, New Zealand. They dangle sticky, shining threads to catch prey. Each worm is only 1 inch (2.5 cm) long. But together, they are very bright. You could easily read by their blue glow.

People can ride boats to visit the glowworms. No talking is allowed, though. If the worms hear one sound, they turn off their lights!

The brightest land animal is the *cucujo* (kuh-KOO-joe), a South American beetle. The cucujo's light stays on all the time. Native people sometimes cage these 2-inch (5-cm) bugs and use them as lamps. Just five cucujos can light up a room.

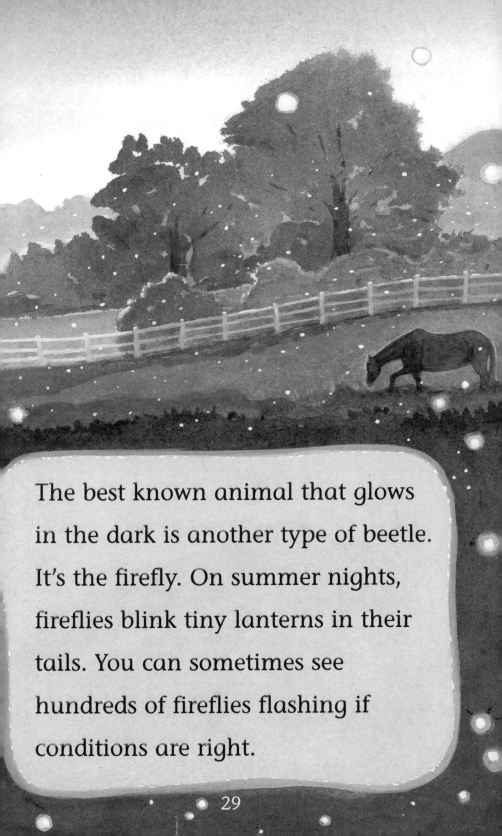

The best known animal that glows in the dark is another type of beetle. It's the firefly. On summer nights, fireflies blink tiny lanterns in their tails. You can sometimes see hundreds of fireflies flashing if conditions are right.

A male firefly blinks his lantern very carefully. If he does it correctly, at just the right speed, a female may blink back. The two fireflies signal back and forth until they find each other.

Catch a firefly on a warm evening. If you are gentle, the firefly may blink for you. You're holding one of nature's living lights!

Index